The Pleasures of Childhood

The Pleasures of Childhood

Edited by Gail Harvey

Gramercy Books

New York • Avenel, New Jersey

Introduction and Compilation
Copyright © 1992 by Outlet Book Company, Inc.
All rights reserved
First published in 1992 by Gramercy Books
distributed by Outlet Book Company, Inc.,
a Random House Company,
40 Engelhard Avenue
Avenel, New Jersey 07001

Manufactured in Hong Kong

Designed by Melissa Ring

Library of Congress Cataloging-in-Publication Data
The Pleasures of childhood.
p.   cm.
ISBN 0-517-07753-1
1. Children—Literary collections.
PN6071.C5P58   1992
820.8′09282—dc20   91-40380   CIP

8 7 6 5 4 3 2 1

Introduction

Childhood—an all too short period of innocence and wonder, of exploration and discovery—has always interested and inspired poets and novelists. Many recount and embellish incidents that occurred during their own childhoods. Others express their feelings for special children they have known. Some search for the adults they are in the children they were.

The Pleasures of Childhood is a delightful collection of poems and prose, written by some of the world's great writers. Louisa May Alcott, for example, tells of the joyous, golden days of her own childhood in Concord, Massachusetts. In two sonnets, the novelist George Eliot (the pseudonym of Mary Ann Evans) tells of her childhood relationship with her brother Isaac Evans. Mark Twain (Samuel Clemens) writes of his boyhood ambition to be a steamboatman on the Mississippi. And John Adams, the second president of the United States, recalls his dislike of school and the pleasures of play. Included, too, are poems by such well-known writers as Robert Louis Stevenson, John Greenleaf Whittier, Christina Rossetti, and Henry Wadsworth Longfellow.

This lovely book, with its charming illustrations, many by Jessie Willcox Smith, will surely awaken warm memories and strike a chord in everyone who reads and rereads it.

GAIL HARVEY

New York
1992

ANSWER TO A CHILD'S QUESTION

Do you ask what the birds say? The sparrow, the dove,
The linnet, and thrush say, "I love and I love!"
In the winter they're silent, the wind is so strong;
What it says I don't know, but it sings a loud song.
But green leaves and blossoms, and sunny warm weather,
And singing and loving, all come back together;
Then the lark is so brimful of gladness and love,
The green fields below him, the blue sky above,
That he sings and he sings and forever sings he,
"I love my love and my love loves me."

SAMUEL TAYLOR COLERIDGE

CRADLE SONG

Sleep, sleep, beauty bright,
Dreaming in the joys of night;
Sleep, sleep; in thy sleep
Little sorrows sit and weep.

Sweet babe, in thy face
Soft desires I can trace,
Secret joys and secret smiles,
Little pretty infant wiles.

As thy softest limbs I feel
Smiles as of the morning steal
O'er thy cheek, and o'er thy breast
Where thy little heart doth rest.

O the cunning wiles that creep
In thy little heart asleep!
When thy little heart doth wake,
Then the dreadful night shall break.

WILLIAM BLAKE

My child is a Phenomenon, really the most wonderful Natural Production I ever beheld. . . .

Lady Holland, famous hostess and great wit of nineteenth-century London

I have got a new-born sister;
I was nigh the first that kissed her.
When the nursing woman brought her
To papa, his infant daughter,
How papa's dear eyes did glisten!—
She will shortly be to christen:
And papa has made the offer,
I shall have the naming of her.
Now I wonder what would please her,
Charlotte, Julia, or Louisa?
Ann and Mary, they're too common;
Joan's too formal for a woman;
Jane's a prettier name beside;
But we had a Jane that died.
They would say, if 'twas Rebecca,

That she was a little Quaker.
Edith's pretty, but that looks
Better in old English books;
Ellen's left off long ago;
Blanche is out of fashion now.
None that I have named as yet
Are so good as Margaret.
Emily is neat and fine.
What do you think of Caroline?
How I'm puzzled and perplext
What to choose or think of next!
I am in a little fever
Lest the name that I shall give her
Should disgrace her or defame her;
I will leave papa to name her.

CHARLES LAMB

My name-son, a bright and blue-eyed rogue, with flaxen hair, screams and laughs like an April morning; and the baby is that species of dough which is called a fine baby.

Sir Walter Scott, Scottish writer, about his grandchildren

When the first baby laughed for the first time, the laugh broke into a thousand pieces and they all went skipping about, and that was the beginning of fairies.

From *Peter Pan* by James Barrie

This little girl, our darling, is become a most intelligent creature, and as gay as a lark, and that in the morning, too, which I do not find so convenient.

Mary Wollstonecraft, the early British feminist writer, to her American lover Gilbert Imlay, about their child

Is there, when the winds are singing
  In the happy summer time,—
When the raptured air is ringing
With Earth's music heavenward springing,
  Forest chirp, and village chime,
Is there, of the sounds that float
Unsighingly, a single note
Half so sweet, and clear, and wild,
As the laughter of a child?

LAMAN BLANCHARD

When Letty had scarce pass'd her third glad year,
And her young, artless words began to flow,
One day we gave the child a color'd sphere
Of the wide earth, that she might mark and know,
By tint and outline, all its sea and land.
She patted all the world; old empires peep'd
Between her baby fingers; her soft hand
Was welcome at all frontiers. How she leap'd,
And laugh'd and prattled in her world-wide bliss;
But when we turned her sweet unlearned eye
On our own isle, she raised a joyous cry,
"Oh! yes, I see it, Letty's home is there!"
And, while she hid all England with a kiss,
Bright over Europe fell her golden hair.

CHARLES TURNER

*N*o one ever keeps a secret as well as a child.

Victor Hugo

JESSIE WILLCOX SMITH.

*T*here's no dew left on the daisies and clover,
  There's no rain left in heaven;
I've said my "seven times" over and over—
  Seven times one are seven.

I am old! so old I can write a letter;
  My birthday lessons are done:
The lambs play always, they know no better;
  They are only one times one.

O Columbine! open your folded wrapper
  Where two twin turtle-doves dwell;
O Cuckoo-pint! toll me the purple clapper,
  That hangs in your clear, green bell.

And show me your nest with the young ones in it—
  I will not steal them away,
I am old! you may trust me, Linnet, Linnet,—
  I am seven times one today.

JEAN INGELOW

THE CHILDREN'S HOUR

Between the dark and the daylight,
  When the night is beginning to lower,
Comes a pause in the day's occupations,
  That is known as the Children's Hour.

I hear in the chamber above me
  The patter of little feet,
The sound of a door that is opened,
  And voices soft and sweet.

From my study I see in the lamplight,
　　Descending the broad hall stair,
Grave Alice, and laughing Allegra,
　　And Edith with golden hair.

A whisper, and then a silence:
　　Yet I know by their merry eyes
They are plotting and planning together
　　To take me by surprise.

A sudden rush from the stairway,
　　A sudden raid from the hall!
By three doors left unguarded
　　They enter my castle wall!

They climb up into my turret
　　O'er the arms and back of my chair;
If I try to escape, they surround me;
　　They seem to be everywhere.

They almost devour me with kisses,
　　Their arms about me entwine,
Till I think of the Bishop of Bingen
　　In his Mouse-Tower on the Rhine!

Do you think, O blue-eyed banditti,
　　Because you have scaled the wall,
Such an old mustache as I am
　　Is not a match for you all!

I have you fast in my fortress,
　　And will not let you depart,
But put you down into the dungeon
　　In the round-tower of my heart.

And there will I keep you forever,
　　Yes, forever and a day,
Till the walls shall crumble to ruin,
　　And moulder in dust away.

HENRY WADSWORTH LONGFELLOW

It is very exciting—the extreme potency of your brats; they might have been nincompoops instead of bubbling and boiling and frizzling like so many pans of sausages on the fire.

Virginia Woolf, English writer, about her nephews, Julian and Quentin Bell, in a letter to her sister Vanessa

I was sent to the public School close by the Stone Church, then kept by Mr. Joseph Cleverly, who died this Year 1802 at the Age of Ninety. Mr. Cleverly was through his whole Life the most indolent Man I ever knew (*excepting Mr. Wibirt*) though a tolerable Schollar and a Gentleman. His inattention to his Schollars was such as gave me a disgust to Schools, to books and to study and I spent my time as idle Children do in making and sailing boats and Ships upon the Ponds and Brooks, in making and flying Kites, in driving hoops, playing marbles, playing Quoits, Wrestling, Swimming, Skaiting and above all in shooting, to which Diversion I was addicted to a degree of Ardor which I know not that I ever felt for any other Business, Study or Amusement.

John Adams, second president of the United States

I copied him, I loved him, I wanted to be him.

Leo Tolstoi, Russian author, about his brother Sergei

*F*or there is no friend like a sister

In calm or stormy weather;

To cheer one on the tedious way,

To fetch one if one goes astray,

To lift one if one totters down,

To strengthen whilst one stands.

Christina Rossetti, English poet,
to her sister Maria Francesca,
who entered an Anglican sisterhood.

I cannot choose but think upon the time
When our two lives grew like two buds that kiss
At lightest thrill from the bee's swinging chime,
Because the one so near the other is.

He was the elder and a little man
Of forty inches, bound to show no dread,
And I the girl that puppy-like now ran,
Now lagged behind my brother's larger tread.

I held him wise, and when he talked to me
Of snakes and birds, and which God loved the best,
I thought his knowledge marked the boundary
Where men grew blind, though angels knew the rest.

If he said "Hush!" I tried to hold my breath;
Wherever he said "Come!" I stepped in faith.

GEORGE ELIOT

One of my earliest memories is of playing with books in my father's study. Building towers and bridges of the big dictionaries, looking at pictures, pretending to read, and scribbling on blank pages whenever pen or pencil could be found. Many of these first attempts at authorship still exist, and I often wonder if these childish plays did not influence my after life, since books have been my greatest comfort, castle-building a never-failing delight, and scribbling a very profitable amusement.

Louisa May Alcott

*H*ow do you like to go up in a swing,
　　Up in the air so blue?
Oh, I do think it the pleasantest thing
　　Ever a child can do!

Up in the air and over the wall,
　　Till I can see so wide,
Rivers and trees and cattle and all
　　Over the countryside—

Till I look down on the garden green,
　　Down on the roof so brown—
Up in the air I go flying again,
　　Up in the air and down!

ROBERT LOUIS STEVENSON

I once had a sweet little doll, dears,
  The prettiest doll in the world;
Her cheeks were so red and so white, dears,
  And her hair was so charmingly curled.
But I lost my poor little doll, dears,
  As I played on the heath one day;
And I cried for her more than a week, dears,
  But I never could find where she lay.

I found my poor little doll, dears,
  As I played on the heath one day;
Folks say she is terribly changed, dears,
  For her paint is all washed away,
And her arms trodden off by the cows, dears,
  And her hair not the least bit curled:
Yet for old sakes' sake she is still, dears,
  The prettiest doll in the world.

CHARLES KINGSLEY

𝒴ou'd scarce expect one of my age
To speak in public on the stage,
And if I chance to fall below
Demosthenes or Cicero,
Don't view me with a critic's eye,
But pass my imperfections by.
Large streams from little fountains flow,
Tall oaks from little acorns grow;
And though now I am small and young,
Of judgment weak and feeble tongue,
Yet all great, learned men, like me
Once learned to read their ABC.

DAVID EVERETT

When I was a boy, there was but one permanent ambition among my comrades in our village on the west bank of the Mississippi River. That was, to be a steamboatman. We had transient ambitions of other sorts, but they were only transient. When a circus came and went, it left us all burning to become clowns; the first Negro minstrel show that ever came to our section left us all suffering to try that kind of life; now and then we had a hope that, if we lived and were good, God would permit us to be pirates. These ambitions faded out, each in its turn; but the ambition to be a steamboatman always remained.

Samuel Clemens (Mark Twain)

*B*lessings on thee, little man,
Barefoot boy, with cheek of tan!
With thy turned-up pantaloons,
And thy merry whistled tunes;
With thy red lip, redder still
Kissed by strawberries on the hill;
With the sunshine on thy face,
Through thy torn brim's jaunty grace;
From my heart I give thee joy,—
I was once a barefoot boy!
Prince thou art,—the grown-up man
Only is republican.
Let the million-dollared ride!
Barefoot, trudging at his side,
Thou hast more than he can buy
In the reach of ear and eye,—
Outward sunshine, inward joy:
Blessings on thee, barefoot boy!

JOHN GREENLEAF WHITTIER

Where the pools are bright and deep,
Where the gray trout lies asleep,
Up the river and over the lea,
That's the way for Billy and me.

Where the blackbird sings the latest,
Where the hawthorn blooms the sweetest,
Where the nestlings chirp and flee,
That's the way for Billy and me.

Where the mowers mow the cleanest,
Where the hay lies thick and greenest,
There to track the homeward bee,
That's the way for Billy and me.

Where the hazel bank is steepest,
Where the shadow falls the deepest,
Where the clustering nuts fall free,
That's the way for Billy and me.

Why the boys should drive away
Little sweet maidens from the play,
Or love to banter and fight so well,
That's the thing I never could tell.

But this I know, I love to play
Through the meadow, among the hay,
Up the water and over the lea,
That's the way for Billy and me.

James Hood

*T*hose Concord days were the happiest of my life, for we had charming playmates in the little Emersons, Channings, Hawthornes and Goodwins, with the illustrious parents and their friends to enjoy our pranks and share our excursions.

Plays in the barn were a favorite amusement, and we dramatized the fairy tales in great style. Our giant came tumbling off a loft when Jack cut down the squash vine running up a ladder to represent the immortal bean. Cinderella rolled away in a vast pumpkin, and a long, black pudding was lowered by invisible hands to fasten itself on the nose of the woman who wanted her three wishes.

Little pilgrims journeyed over the hills with scrip and staff and cockle-shells in their hats; elves held their pretty revels among the pines, and "Peter Wilkins'" flying ladies came swinging down on the birch tree-tops. Lords and ladies haunted the garden, and mermaids splashed in the bath-house of woven willows over the brook.

Louisa May Alcott

Respect the child. Be not too much his parent. Trespass not on his solitude.

Ralph Waldo Emerson

Children's playings are not sports and should be deemed as their most serious actions.

Michel Eyquem de Montaigne

The childhood shows the man

As morning shows the day.

John Milton

*S*weet childish days, that were as long

As twenty days are now.

William Wordsworth

All night long and every night,
When my mamma puts out the light,
I see the people marching by
As plain as day, before my eye.

Armies and emperors and kings,
All carrying different kinds of things,
And marching in so grand a way,
You never saw the like by day
So fine a show was never seen
At the great circus on the green:
For every kind of beast and man
Is marching in that caravan.

At first they move a little slow,
But still the faster on they go,
And still beside them close I keep
Until we reach the town of Sleep.

ROBERT LOUIS STEVENSON

When all the world is young, lad,
 And all the trees are green;
And every goose a swan, lad,
 And every lass a queen;
Then hey for boot and horse, lad,
 And round the world away;
Young blood must have its course, lad,
 And every dog his day.

When all the world is old, lad,
 And all the trees are brown;
And all the sport is stale, lad,
 And all the wheels run down:
Creep home, and take your place there,
 The spent and maimed among:
God grant you find one face there
 You loved when all was young.

CHARLES KINGSLEY

She pictured to herself how this same little sister of hers would, in the after-time, be herself a grown woman; and how she would keep, through all her riper years, the simple and loving heart of her childhood: and how she would gather about her other little children, and make *their* eyes bright and eager with many a strange tale, perhaps even with the dream of Wonderland of long-ago: and how she would feel with all their simple sorrows, and find a pleasure in all their simple joys, remembering her own child-life and the happy summer days.

—*From* Alice in Wonderland
by Lewis Carroll

Twinkle, twinkle, little star,
How I wonder what you are!
Up above the world so high,
Like a diamond in the sky.

When the blazing sun is gone,
When he nothing shines upon,
Then you show your little light,
Twinkle, twinkle, all the night.

Then the traveler in the dark
Thanks you for your tiny spark:
He could not see which way to go,
If you did not twinkle so.

In the dark-blue sky you keep,
And often through my curtains peep,
For you never shut your eye
Till the sun is in the sky.

As your bright and tiny spark
Lights the traveler in the dark,
Though I know not what you are,
Twinkle, twinkle, little star.

JANE TAYLOR

When I was a child, I spake as a child,
I understood as a child, I thought as a child:
but when I became a man I put away
childish things.

I Corinthians 13:11

$\mathcal{C}$hildren have neither past nor future; they enjoy the present, which very few of us do.

Jean de La Bruyère

School parted us; we never found again
That childish world where our two spirits mingled
Like scents from varying roses that remain
One sweetness, nor can evermore be singled.

Yet the twin habit of that early time
Lingered for long about the heart and tongue:
We had been natives of one happy clime,
And its dear accent to our utterance clung,

Till the dire years whose awful name is Change
Had grasped our souls still yearning in divorce,
And pitiless shaped them in two forms that range
Two elements which sever their life's course.

But were another childhood-world my share,
I would be born a little sister there.

GEORGE ELIOT

*B*ack, turn backward, O Time, in thy flight;

Make me a child again, just for tonight.

Elizabeth Akers Allen

*H*ow dear to my heart are the scenes of my childhood,
  When fond recollection presents them to view!
The orchard, the meadow, the deep tangled wildwood,
  And every loved spot which my infancy knew,
The wide-spreading pond and the mill that stood by it,
  The bridge and the rock where the cataract fell;
The cot of my father, the dairy house nigh it,
  And e'en the rude bucket that hung in the well.

That moss-covered bucket I hailed as a treasure,
  For often at noon, when returned from the field,
I found it the source of an exquisite pleasure,
  The purest and sweetest that nature can yield.
How ardent I seized it, with hands that were glowing,
  And quick to the white-pebbled bottom it fell.
Then soon, with the emblem of truth overflowing,
  And dripping with coolness, it rose from the well.

How sweet from the green, mossy brim to receive it,
    As, poised on the curb, it inclined to my lips!
Not a full, blushing goblet could tempt me to leave it,
    Tho' filled with the nectar that Jupiter sips.
And now, far removed from the loved habitation,
    The tear of regret will intrusively swell,
As fancy reverts to my father's plantation,
    And sighs for the bucket that hung in the well.

SAMUEL WOODWORTH

I played with you 'mid cowslips blowing,
When I was six and you were four;
When garlands weaving, flower-balls throwing,
Were pleasures soon to please no more.
Through groves and meads, o'er grass and heather,
With little playmates, to and fro,
We wandered hand in hand together;
But that was sixty years ago.

T. L. PEACOCK